Is MORNING SURE?

Poems by

LAURA BENÉT

The Odyssey Press « 1947 » New York

PRINTED IN THE UNITED STATES

FIRST EDITION

To

STEPHEN VINCENT BENÉT

with the love that is old, and the

admiration that is continually new

ACKNOWLEDGMENTS

THE AUTHOR gratefully acknowledges permission from *Voices* to reprint "Felicity's Meadow," "Flier Over New Hampshire Valley," "To F. R. B.," and "Rosamond's Maze"; from the Washington *Post* to reprint "Face of the Waters"; from the *Christian Science Monitor* to reprint "Privet Hedge"; from the *Saturday Review of Literature* to reprint "Middle Age," "To Lola Ridge," "Silence to the Poet," "Wind Woman," "Any Soldier," "Is Morning Sure?" and "Child Light"; from the New York *Sun* to reprint "Sixty Seconds"; from the New York *Times* to reprint "The Crown," "Snow Lover," "The Frantic Steed," "Slim Foot," and "New York Dawn"; from *Commonweal* to reprint "The Cell"; from *America* to reprint "Town Character," "Dear Wound," "Old Man in the Country," "The Stranger," "Salvation," "Rainbow," and "Out of Bounds"; from *Poetry: A Magazine of Verse* to reprint "Rulers"; and from "Poetry Lane" of the *National Parent-Teacher Magazine* to reprint "The Fighter" and "Impossible Love." Also from Earle Thomas for the use of "Deer in Time of War" and "Intermezzo," which appeared in his column "Through the Arch" in *The Villager*; from the *North Georgia Review* to reprint "Portrait"; and from Margery Mansfield to reprint "A Lady's A.B.C.," which was published in her anthology, *American Women Poets*, 1937.

L. B.

CONTENTS

IS MORNING SURE?

DEER IN TIME OF WAR

The deer are here again—
Agile and innocent,
Candid as growing grain;
At a dark moment sent,
In a world given to pain,
Young deer appear again.

Their fawns are come to graze,
As delicate children go
On unknown winding ways
Not even hunters know.
If they stray, wholly lost,
Lush grass was worth the cost.

Sensitive as young love,
Velvety, wonder-eyed,
Cherished as in a grove
From brutes far and wide,
Suspecting nothing born
Of cruelty and scorn.

O be rarely viewed—
Like phantoms disappear,
Only at night renewed!
Man's the beast, not deer,
And you the ghostly spirit
He never may inherit.

FACE OF THE WATERS

Like a child the water ran
In the great experiment
When the universe began.
Over new-made firmament
Chased and raced a growing flood
To the very feet of God.

And God, smiling and at ease,
Saw this fresh interpreter
Winding through the leafy trees,
Wetting all the creatures' fur
Like a bright evangelist
Whose disciples must be kissed.

Water emulated sky,
Water carried voice of birds,
Crawling beasts from covert nigh
Lapped of it in grateful herds.
Sorely had the infant earth
Thirsted since its hour of birth.

"Water," cried the weary Lord,
"Be the medicine of sight!
You, the shining, silver cord
With a living gift alight,
Shall attain a holiness
Rooted things forever miss.

"In long days' monotony
Man, the wandering alien,
Listens to clear melody,
Kneeling in some grassy glen
Where your course is toward the sea
And his dream, Eternity."

IS MORNING SURE?

(New Hampshire Village, 5 A.M.)

Here is the dark of sunken country earth,
Like the deep grave, a close-mouthed, silent bed,
No flicker in any house of light's rebirth—
One village has surrendered to the dead.

When man emerges slowly, he is gone,
A phantom blanketed in windy cold.
Usurping night so jealous of the dawn,
Watches her as a wolf a sleeping fold.

Only the cocks are rallying. Their cries
Lose triumph, echo needle-thin and poor:
"Will that ball, yellow as barnyard corn, arise
Again?" they seem to shrill. "Is morning sure?"

SLIM FOOT

I know a meadow
Where light is dim.
Poppy flowers
Burn at its rim,
Doves cry drowsily,
Streams lie still,
Brown head to gold head
Nods at will.

To reach that meadow,
O child of grace,
Let lacy spider web
Cover your face.
Lay your hand on the root
By the rose-thorn hedge—
And-your-slim-foot-
Goes-over-its-edge!

CHILD LIGHT

O light, so excellent, so gently good,
Bestowed like a libation on the earth,
A freshening dew upon the desperate heart,
The golden certainty of daily birth.

Your apparition in the quickened East
Is a bright trumpet for a valiant soul;
Silent and hopeless, we were aliens here,
If over us an ocean's night should roll.

You rose upon the first green mysteries,
Primeval leaves and uncouth, clumsy beasts;
You were the kernel in the swelling grain,
The burning carpet for a million feasts.

With you ten thousand visions fill man's brain,
The dying and condemned acclaim your ray;
You warm the eyelids of the patient blind,
Bringing the transient kindliness of day.

A luminous arm outstretched, protesting death,
Signs our release from Dark's reluctant stream.
Light, like an innocent and trustful child,
You smile above each newly buried dream.

A LADY'S A.B.C.

That was a peacock, my lady,
Strutting your garden.
We praised the daintiness strayed
From a forest of Arden,
In whose plumage of many colors
A rainbow broke—
No one would have said, "A peacock!"
Till the harsh scream spoke.

That was a horned toad hidden
In your mind's domain,
Gorging itself on ego's
Fat drops of rain.
Swelling to size full double—
Braggadocio
Burst the skin! Such trouble
For an overthrow.

There was a subtle serpent
Jealousy nourished
On the choicest of the apples
A green tree flourished.
"Only a mottled necklace
Without a fang,"
You murmured, feeling no venom
Till it coiled, and sprang.

WIND WOMAN

Wind seeks a habitation. Once a girl
Bound out to service, lonely, unbelieving,
Committed her frail spirit to the air,
Weary of earthly sorrow and long grieving.

On March nights she stands tall against the stars,
From their far kingdom draws a passing gleam
Called hope; then rushes on throughout the waste,
Shrilling her fear to hill and icy stream.

With youngling April, this sad, vagrant one
Grows calmer and her robe less wildly waves;
Like bird and insect, winter penance done,
She gains warm pasture, squirrels' leafy caves.

In the fast-greening bushes, hums a song,
Changed from a phantom only born to weep
To a breeze, merry-murmuring yet strong,
And in some new-built nest, soon falls asleep.

PRIVET HEDGE

Since life decrees that all things grow
According to their own design,
Require not of a meek hedgerow
The virtue of a climbing vine.

Yet Nature's conscience weighs the cost.
The thrifty hedge attains a goal;
Granted it be not thinned by frost
Or ravaged by a reckless mole.

Plant one; and, as the seasons ride,
An imperceptible slow rise
Like gently swelling river tide
Steals upon your astonished eyes.

Until one year the flowering bands
Tower above your new-set trees,
And small grandchildren lift their hands
To blossoms first-claimed by the bees.

TOWN CHARACTER

Say this of Hope, a visiting spinster,
Familiar nurse, whose form we know,
Her garment bears a charm for danger
    (Flower on newly fallen snow).

Yet Hope, continually shabby,
Slips beggarlike along the street,
So slight the burden of her presence,
Ghostlike her charitable feet,

From a deep basket, doling ribbons,
Herbs and green wreaths with special grace;
And there be those among the aging
Live but to look upon her face,

When like a maid come from her attic,
Attentive to the feeblest sound,
More often in some antechamber,
She tends a gnawing, constant wound.

Dismissed but ever freshly summoned,
Skilled in long waiting, brightly shy,
Through centuries of willing service,
Grown so young she cannot die.

ONE VOICE

O to hear the one voice,
The organ exultant,
Familiar, resilient
That made us rejoice;
To hear again the fond tone,
The low tone, the loved one,
Calling up the stair,
Coming out of the air!

Let us hear the voice
That gladdened our dawnings,
Building true mornings
As we opened the door.
Words of an enchanted joy,
Speech of muted sorrow—
They dignified the morrow
When mirth was no more.

The incomparable voice—
Why must it be silent?
We wait, we hunger dumbly
For its welcoming praise.
Will it come in a far hour
When the spirit gathers power?
Does some strong wind retain it
Blowing over our days?

PORTRAIT

Eager for love that is not lean,
Life that gives unreservedly,
Her fervent eyes survey the scene
With boundless curiosity,

A lodging house her only nest.
Flapping deaf ears to lose no word,
Neighbors regard her as a pest,
A fluttering, incessant bird.

A bird that preys upon their hive
To pick up shreds of daily meat,
On endless chattering to thrive,
Its eggs hatched in another's heat.

With "What I saw" and "Where I went,"
As uneventful years roll on,
Her longing is for riches spent—
Licking a salt whose savor's gone.

Relatives run; those of more grace
Evade her queries as they may,
Yet in a glazed and cheated face,
Youth's avid eyes devour the day.

DEAR WOUND

"A dangerous wound to cure!"
The tattlers sighed,
"How can she thus endure?
The gash is wide,
May drugs insure
No bleeding from the side."

"Let it not swiftly heal,"
Spoke one more just,
"Lest a live hurt congeal
Into a crust,
Impervious to the feel
Of ache or thrust."

"Beloved wound"—
(The woman felt it burn),
"What theories they propound,
Where may they turn
Dulling for me this pain?
O malady
Whose healing is in vain,
Dead I should be
Without my constant rain
Of agony!"

SILENCE AND THE POET

Compelling mantle of night air
He felt; maternal tenderness
Wrapped him around. With leaves to bless
She wove his darkly heavy hair.

He who had chanted of the world,
Heard trumpets breathe from ramparts, now
Lay still, her hand upon his brow,
Slumbering, his proud banners furled.

The words he would have written fled
Like mating larks from out his room.
He did not need its healing gloom
To drive them from his weary head.

"Be now my witness," Silence cried,
"And I shall tame both pen and tongue.
No syllable if said or sung
Shall occupy them while I bide.

"Sounding the scale of soundless hymns,
You shall transcend the planes of space,
Viewing Medusa's quelling face
Where, in the void, her island swims;

"The infinite you shall daily know
Until the finite fades. At last,
Emerging from the muted past
Attirèd in a light like snow,

"Speech will return like new-sprung flowers;
Humans like angels share your road;
You liberated from the load
That shackled your immortal powers."

OUT OF BOUNDS

Allow not reason's gates to hedge
Her world so vivid and so pure,
Wherein clear lakes and mountain ledge
Make toiling progress free and sure.

Mind takes the highroad. It is meet
That spirit sway the pulsing air,
Where wonder, scorning cautious feet,
Bridges dim chaos by a hair.

Bind her not to narrow sight,
Spilling her aims to time and space.
Who would desire a falcon's flight
Be measured in a heavenly race?

ANY SOLDIER

Irrevocably lost, his mind
Resigned itself in desperate calm.
It seemed as though catastrophe
Were freighted with a subtle balm;

As though the flying ice and sleet
Cleansed him of life's tormenting claim.
Their coldness was an antidote
More purifying than quick flame.

Strangely, war seemed inconsequent.
Now he had challenged blood and fire,
Such peace was his as lights on those
Who sacrifice their own desire.

He found within his startled self
The reason for man's birth and death,
Not knowing where he was in time,
About to forfeit sight and breath.

FLIER OVER NEW HAMPSHIRE VALLEY

Poised giddily in the blue air,
His bloodshot eyes discerned below
A flowing valley's contours grow.
Young memory was buried there.

Instant upon the mind this place
Sprang into being; he had swung
Rod over ripple's lashing tongue
In heady fathoms of the race.

That river winked at roving wiles,
Since berries grew in bushy glade;
Knee-deep he had been wont to wade
The generous lap of water miles.

Fear gripped him as the plane whirled down.
Swift fate was numbing to the sense,
A chilly twilight darkly dense;
Yet boyhood courage claimed its own.

Plane was to sink and pilot die—
Where better might his heart be stilled?
What other realm so well fulfilled
As earth, his far-sought destiny?

THE COMPANION

A shadow falls upon the glade.
Across clear vision of delight
Strides the tall dusk. Man is afraid
Of one companion called the night.

The shadow cleaves to him. That dark
Presence with wisdom in its eye,
He must revere as friend, and mark
Its counsel as the years go by.

With age it grows in substance. Soon
Twin light and shade blend into gray.
Lightning may strike down at noon;
Chameleon dawn may rise to slay;

But in his ear a muted voice
Sings one cold flood's not alien foam;
Styx, known river of his choice,
Goes murmuring by the lights of home.

SIXTY SECONDS

Hang not on circuit of Time's wheel,
But realize, with head uplifted,
That sixty seconds' flight is gifted
With all the heart may ever feel.

Light minute, strung on golden wires,
Delicate as antennaed nerve,
With what velocity you serve
To flash the subterranean fires!

Tiniest unit, covered thick
With symbols written in new blood,
Your slight inexorable tick
Stems and defies Time's river-flood.

NEW YORK DAWN

The iron city is still and locked in sleep.
Men's wishes—power, money, desired good—
Sink to oblivion in this lesser death,
Even the need of shelter and of food.

In the interval between a darkened void
And the returning light, there reigns supreme
A tranquil kingdom where man may escape
His goading torment through the web of dream.

His childhood angel drawing near to him,
Bears like green branches signs of spring and sea.
In that unconscious joy he drops the beast
And recognizes clear infinity.

The alarm peals forth. Inexorable Time
Like the death watch's sharply ticking beat . . .
He snatches at his coat. There are the stairs
Leading him to the tom-toms of the street.

THE CROWN

Crown us who make within
Our thrones and places high.
Though the gold crown be thin,
Let it be light as sky.

And may the aureole shine,
The rounded circlet glow,
That we be kings in fine
Before our overthrow.

One crown, one life, one hour—
Decree in justice, Lord,
That none usurp the power
Of our so brief award!

RAINBOW

Strangely to him the rain brought peace
Where he believed peace could not fall.
On pain's dark flood with no surcease,
Relief came with the rain's soft call.

Dropping from lips all limpid light,
Those syllables awakened song,
Lilting in childhood vaguely bright,
Remembered long ago and long.

"A godly thing," she crooned, "to weep,
Water brings springing vine from stone,
Yet not within your soul to creep
As a lion wounded and alone.

"Once ocean, green earth holds her hands
To welcome tears. Then let them flow,
Rather than still the breast with bands
To silence life like numbing snow.

"Tears are of joy; joy born of tears
As surely as a flower from sun,
To cloven rock resign your fears,
Look on the rainbow once begun!"

SNOW LOVER

Upon the form of wondering earth
Descends as subtle a caress
As seventh sense might bring to birth
In consummating loveliness.

No courtier in the ages' race
Ever enfolded his delight
In so ethereal an embrace,
A garment of such glistening white.

From soundless country he is come,
His footfall and his lips are mute,
Barren enchantment left her dumb,
Lost in a silence absolute.

Lonely, she shyly gropes for heaven,
Snow covers her! In mild surprise
Confidence is wholly given
As when Eve saw her lover's eyes.

THE CELL

Retreat within this room,
And searching, find
No murmur of a loom,
No comforts kind.

The window panes hold dust,
The chair is hard,
Candlestick red with rust,
A shutter barred.

What penury! No light
Nor shred of food—
Denied the anchorite
All earthly good?

Yes, by a strange decree,
But rest within.
Sit silently
And sunshine will begin

To gild its center,
Tawny birds fly forth,
Presences enter
Of a singular worth.

This niche so bleakly thin
Of pinching dole,
Is the good inn
Of the restless soul.

DESPERATE REMEDY

In the dull cottage once again,
Golden notes brush the cobwebbed wall;
A singing bird threads a refrain
Innocent as a fountain's fall.

Let not the bird that sings so sweet,
Lilting, lift too high his trill;
There may come padding on clawed feet,
Envy, a cat that laps ill-will.

Tie down the radiant, soaring wings
Of Happiness, deny him bread;
Even his simple maunderings
Shall rouse the sparrows overhead,

Those jealous beggars, bearing grief,
That limping starling, rusty Care;
Rather for your soul's relief
Fling wide the cage to wintry air,

Wave the flying joy farewell,
Kneeling before a sobered hearth,
Lest creatures darkly infidel
Defile a lustrous form with earth.

A STRANGER

Here stands in grotesque garments, one
Whom suns have traveled to create,
Slow-crawling cells fought for and won
In misty caverns inchoate.

Within him ticks a little heart,
A little mind. Dread memories keep
His acts from being wholly blind,
His being desperately asleep.

Some fringe of the benignant skies
Grazed him when consciousness began,
Upon amazing scenes new eyes
Fed long ere he became a man.

Now tunneled subway, glib machine
Claim him: to sordidness is bowed
Spirit whose heritage had been
The essence of a flaming cloud.

Yet subjugated flesh has breathed
At moments, a divining thing,
Victorious pity, crowned and wreathed
Like the sure triumph of the Spring.

MIDDLE AGE

Deep in the wood it is not well
To follow the elusive sun,
Or to anticipate a trail
Where young deer fleetly timid run.

The herbal wood holds memory's dove,
Rings multiply on aging trees,
Sweating desire one's soul to prove
Sinks into hermit's musing ease.

Once when the lightning flared, we leapt,
Where thunder rolled our ardent cry
The banner of a legion swept,
Bidding ten thousand rise and die.

Now the soft twilight wood allures
A young bird's faintly bubbling tone
Enough. What is it that endures,
Integral as this boulder stone?

THE TRAITOR

A white stone in her father's field
Had marked the goal of failing sight.
Precarious rays of sunset light
Were by its snowy luster sealed.

So when her eyes rebellious grew,
Deborah on an autumn walk
Gauged by the upturned boulder's chalk,
And not the fiery maples' hue

The fading power of her eyes.
One shining stone a comrade stood
To reassure and lift the hood
Veiling her bounteous eager skies.

Then came a winter's night when she
For starry tonic crept outside,
Gazed; found it not. A sentinel's pride
Had bowed before the enemy

And the besieging dark had won
Compelling full surrender now,
Since she had lost, scarce knowing how,
The password of her lucky stone.

DREAM

With you I beheld new land
Where a sphinx's wings unfurled,
Recognized the shifting sand
Of another world,

Knew it to be alien ground
Luminous beings tread.
Aerial moon rays wrapped us round
With a filmy thread.

Plains were glassy, ether rare,
Unseen things had sway,
Who had braved the sickening glare
Of our grilling day.

Twisted tree root, oddly spun,
Served as spying glass;
Through it I gazed out upon
A hidden valley's pass.

Such visions from that chasm rose
I felt a deadly fear;
Never had you clung so close,
Never seemed so dear.

And I fled the cold sublime
For your reality:
"Comrade, what are space and time?
Lift your eyes to me!"

INTERMEZZO

The Macdowell Colony

Flung from the wheel of spinning haste
Into the silence of great space,
Initiated by the chaste
Beauty to which I lift my face,
Hours move at a calmer pace.

How futile the lost world! How good
The casual of every day—
Illusion of the brooding wood
Where even leaves a law obey,
And the unseen holds her sway.

Here we are tossed a second chance
In a circle charmed; and demon time
May not intrude on circumstance.
So we rest and slowly climb
As flowering trees attain their prime.

THE FRANTIC STEED

Hooves of a charger, iron-shod swift Time,
Pause! for the frantic steed is almost spent.
Warfare's a pestilence too often sent;
The courser is no longer in his prime.
Though he may hear metallic summons chime,
He will not whinny. Far behind him lie
Those piteous human heaps, where vultures fly
And every wind's a messenger of crime.

Time, canter out to pasture; let us place
A muzzle on your nose and weight your heels;
Humble as a carter's donkey, droop your face,
Halting your gallop, for this planet reels!
One day you may be vanquished in your race
By the fiery spirits loosing seven seals.

IMPOSSIBLE LOVE

Make haste, dear. Both of us are growing old.
Imagine all the pleasures we may have
Before years hurry us to a dull grave,
Or lightly squandered is the heart's red gold.
Why, there are confidences manifold,
Volumes to scan and idiotic games;
I have your picture in a hundred frames—
You are the white lamb in a swarming fold.
But you must promise faithfulness and grace.
Though calming, let your wind be never cool,
Blowing to weeds my little garden place.
Remember, every lover is a fool.
And if the sum of living be love's fee,
Tremble. You are my one eternity.

TO F. R. B.

In dreams I see you happy—and perceive
Your joyous spirit to be born again
To greater exultation and that gain
None save the truly noble may achieve.
Nor can I ever in my mind conceive
Of you without some souls to entertain,
Your salty mirth's compassionate refrain
Holding no element to wound or grieve.

You come in color! In translucent blue
Of tranquil summer sky, unruffled sea,
Companioned by familiars of your own.
Where meadows of adventure yield no rue,
You rest contented as a blossomy tree,
Through whose new leaves benignant winds have blown.

TO A FIGHTER (S. V. B.)

Laughter was born with you in noonday sun,
And high adventure for your every plan.
The whole of life became a heightened span
When in the clouds you saw a chariot run.
Coursers reared to the sky and gold wheels spun,
Sun-dust was scattered on your lucky head,
Speeding you on in triumph. Early dead
Yet ever living, know your race was won.

How we exulted in your yesterdays
With great processions going toward the sea,
Of brilliant epic and fantastic plays.
Oh, that those intimate joys again could be!
But you sought mightier waters, voyaged far
Beyond Atlantis and the western star.

TO LOLA RIDGE

On nebulous heights long-parted comrades shine.
You tower above them; touch and understand
The flaming revelations of that land
Whose crystal liberty is meat and wine.
Since you were one most instant to divine
Bright gold from unsound metal, your slight hand
And unscathed heart take over the command
Of eager souls marked by the fiery sign.

If in my verse some magic lines emerge
Or wayward syllables with wonder blaze,
Give that encouragement you gave me young;
If poems born of some unconscious urge
Rise up like singing fountains on still days,
They mount on the approval of your tongue.

STONE ON ANOTHER STONE

Man to be saved must trail the ghostly lyre
Of manifold birds, innumerable trees
With the abundance of the blossoms' choir
Whose intricacies yield to prying bees;
Follow the vanishing horse and furtive fawn,
More surely loyal than his savage spark.
Progression shall enfold them in new dawn,
Another world were a diminished arc
Without their lappings and their searchings—what
Is it their lifted muzzles listen for?
Does Man assume that they shall be forgot
Leaving him sole, triumphant conqueror?
Immortal beasts precede the two-legged things
Unheard of in primeval trumpetings.

But somewhere Man, the sage and cannibal,
Swimming entrenchèd seas, hid in a cave,
Aware of incandescence mystical,
A ray of light that flickered on a wave;
Slept in a mountain valley breathed alive
By Alpine dawn; and knew in that lone bowl
A torch was flung by which he might arrive,
A signal lit on a forgotten shoal.
Out of the barrenness there beckoned sun
That he might lay stone on another stone,
Snatching at life, might forward with it run,
He, the uncomprehended hermit one.
In endless circle of immensities
A second sight of prophets burned his eyes.

OLD MAN IN THE COUNTRY

Man who is reared by Nature as he grows
Flees her green skirt for warring throngs until
His latter years draw on—the elder blows
And every hour is weighed with some small ill.
Then She, the never-aging, doling ease
Secure among her herbs and blossoms, calls,
Hides his infirmities by drooping trees.
His querulous voice among her waterfalls
Takes on remembered cadence. Steps once light
Falter at hills that touch indulgent sky,
Whispering his dear secrets to the night,
Retreating to inconsequent infancy
As stature wanes, he stammers with the tongue
Of bird-filled valleys, ever shrilly young.

EXPLORE THE MOON

Should we win through to this far, ghoulish strand
Where life aroused would perish instantly,
With never comrade near to take our hand,
Nor sight of flowering shrub, green bush, or tree,
Would we not shrink or shrivel like grass-blade
Glared on by giants, turn at last to stone
Forgotten in some staring, frightful glade
Until another aeon should come on?
Cold is this planet—cold as an icy heart
That expiates a penance—among stars
Hung as a warning where its rays may dart
Toward old earth teeming with its many wars.
Destroyed by such fey looks, moon's creatures must
Have vanished into something less than dust.

Kindled emotions move like frightened beasts—
For this chill brightness no more truly bright
Than ghosts behind the living at a feast,
Ghouls flitting through a crater's waning light.
Beware the place where quickly coursing blood
Pauses because of a monstrous unseen eye.
What clay survives such unrelenting flood
Of coldness as prevails eternally?
Mountains and valleys are here—many a sign
And symbol of our ruddy, friendly earth
But nothing so fulfilling or benign—
Some secret curse prevailed at the moon's birth.
Silence it has, a silence so profound
The very rocks must groan to hear a sound!

SYLVIA'S SHOES

Sandals shod young Sylvia!
Were ever two feet matched as trim
As Sylvia's dancing on the rim
Of a sunlit world?
Ever heel and toe
More adroitly curled
To come and go?

Thus continually,
In and out and roundabout,
Sylvia floated airily
With never a scowl nor pout,
Apple of the township's eye,
Shod so daintily.

Tripped in middle age
As at blithe sixteen,
Not one whit more sage
Than a fairy queen,
Dreamy as a harebell
Nodding in a pass,
Candid as a well
In the autumn grass.

Whence came her sandal shoes?
Nobody knew.
To their unfading blues
None held the clue.
Orphaned Sylvia dwelt alone
As a singular pure stone.

When she mounted age's
Silver-rimed hill,
Turned yellow pages—
She had no will
Over running feet,
Sandals become rusty;
Into winter sleet,
Into gardens dusty,
Sandals now refused to go,
Petulantly pulled away.
Sandals wished to stay at home—
Woe, woe!

Sylvia old yet fair,
Grieving overmuch,
Lolled upon a rocking chair,
Leaned upon a crutch,
Her throaty voice declining
To a plaintive whining.
Doleful was the hour
When bleak age descended
On that untouched flower!

Then, to town there wended
Strong as a sea-going oar,
A stranger slender-fingered.
In his gear he bore
Colors oddly blended.
And to Sylvia's door he came,
Buoyant as a leaping flame.

She confided straight
Dark alarms and fears
For her sandals' fate.
Beside her cradle placed,
On her ankles laced
By a shape that crossed the room
In birth dawn's uncertain gloom
(So her mother had declared),
Growing as she grew,
Faring as she fared.
All her days she'd worn them—
Must she now disown them?

The painter like a bending rush
Nodded, looked upon their wear,
Wielded his fantastic brush
Finer than a single hair,
Touching sodden shoes with gold
Wreathed in colors manifold.
Lo, sandals tapped the rug again,
Capering upon the floor!

Who was prouder than
Our Sylvia when they bore
Her slender, lissom weight?
Trippingly she glided
With all her wonted state.
Lightfooted she went
Without pain or fear
Over whited door sill—
One, two, three and one.
The seventh night
And candlelight
Was gone from the house on the hill!

* * *

"Not safe to put the sandals on
Once they were gilded!"
Cried a neighbor woman
Telling Sylvia's worth.
"Ah, she put them on, the sweet,
After they were gilded;
Now to heavenly streets
Her creator builded
They have borne her forth,
As a sunlit river
Wandering forever."

RULERS—A PARABLE

The trees going forth on a time
To anoint a king,
Called to the olive in prime,
"Be crowned and sing,
Come and over us lean,
Cool, fragrant, green!"

But the olive shook dusky head
Where the ripe fruit clung,
As slowly he said
With hesitant, careful tongue,
"Forsake my ripeness, whereby
We do honor to One on high;
Desert my olives and oil
For a kingdom's toil?"

The trees then sought out the fig:
"Little friend, be our lord"—
"Leave my fruit to dry on the twig?"
Was the figtree's word.
"My velvety dark delight
That purples the branch tonight,
Would rot and be spoil for bees,
Should I take mine ease."

Despairingly then the trees
Approached to a vine
Fluttering in the breeze,
"Be for us, a sign
And symbol of monarchy,
To rule over every tree!"

"Alas," said the vine, "escape?
Think on wine new-made,
Sweet juices of reddened grape,
And stand dismayed.
Man would miss the lifting draught
Thirsty Adam quaffed,
Cease my vigorous functioning
To be the wood's tame king?"

After long, weary ramble
Trees came in discontent
To a thorny bramble,
Crying, "Our time is spent.
O listen, wandering one,
And come to the throne,
Strengthen our sapling groves
If the spirit moves?"

To the anxious group in the meadow
Stout bramble replied in scorn,
"Can you trust in my threatening shadow,
Suffer pain of my thorn?
Know that fire's deadly leaping
May arouse you from dreams and sleeping,
That sudden flame kindling me
Will devour your greenery?"

The trees departed in haste,
Their leaves shedding sorrow.
There was no king for the morrow,
No ruler to keep their state
Against wind's turbulent hate
Or those subtle enemies
That gnaw in the night at trees—
Since they could not put their faith
In the bramble's rugged girth,
In the bramble's sturdy shadow
Darkening the meadow.

EZEKIEL'S LAMP

In an ancient house
On a quiet street,
Strangely haunted
By unseen feet,
Brooded a window—
As each dusk fell
A lamp was placed
On the window sill,
Beneficent
Against the night.

In the high house, hidden,
Brow-beaten, chidden,
Dwelled Ezekiel,
A craftsman
Cunningly gifted.
The lamp, an offering
To his Celestina.
(Ezekiel was unhappy
With his wife,
Faded and torn
The garment of his life.)

On the night of Celestina's end
She strangely moaned
Of saints and fiery beasts,

Her voice intoned,
"Rivers beside a throne
And gardens painted."
She looked upon the lamp
As it were tainted.
Would it contrive
To watch him tenderly,
She not being by?

"Your virgin and your vestal,"
She muttered acridly.
Words of fantastic pride.

After she died,
Ezekiel spent his days
In workroom, guild;
Yet never came at night
Solitude's chill.
Touched by no hand
The lamp remained alight,
Perpetually bright.

Useless it was for him or any other
To handle it, to touch,
To trim and watch
Whether the wick was high;
In hidden secrecy the lamp burned on.

An evanescent host
A twelvemonth took to fashion her
Who was to be Ezekiel's star.
When at last she hovered over
The lamp as an adoring lover,
Her spirit was as youngest day.
Golden hair all golden lay
About a face like an open flower.
At times she grew tall as a tower,
Ever at night she came and went,
Vanishing with morning's horn—

And he who had been lost, forlorn,
Felt day by day, a gleam
Of deepest happiness.
Never with Celestina
Had he acknowledged bliss.
Like roses climbing
On his carven wood
Came golden good,
What he desired was his.

So lived the lamp, so loved Ezekiel
Many years to tell.

FELICITY'S MEADOW

From the new house that fed her spirit's need
Felicity looked upon a sunny meadow,
Finding far more than meat or drink her meed
The interplaying of its light and shadow.

Runners of autumn tinted the wild grasses
Into the semblance of a tawny hide,
And ever moving, moving flowed the masses
Of blades whose restlessness could not abide

Security of that beloved valley,
Those dappled beeches guarding a quiet glade,
And the wind ceasing not to stir and rally
The desperate surging of each sorrel blade,

Forever straining, quivering, returning.
It seemed the very meadow must expand,
Throughout the summer beckoned ever burning
The lighted target of that fertile land.

Again the shock: safe in her windowed fold
Where there was no rude knocking at her door
And all she loved and touched was hers to hold,
Felicity heard the rumor of a war,

Oceans away. Moving in mild amaze
At this convulsive heaving of a world,
Felicity gave thanks for her calm days,
For spacious quiet cradling her. Unfurled

Before her lay her own deep-rooted holding,
That meadow an inseparable part
Of her soul's self, entrenched and always folding
Back on the circle of her dreamy heart.

Yet was her meadow changed. She could not muster
Belief in such insidious wizardry—
As fall winds came with winter in their bluster
Under a threatening and opaque sky,

The grasses glittered with metallic color,
Like formidable weapons rose in height;
Glancing from doorways in astonished dolor,
Felicity fancied she saw flares at night,

Heard whispers, half commanding and half fawning,
Asking "Which way?" and "At what point?" and "Go!"
Horror was heightened one December dawning
When from her window on the turf below

She saw onrushing, shadowy, silent forces
Trample her loved land where the tawny grass
Had swayed so mildly in the water courses—
Ah, was it possible these shapes would pass

Her fences' paling and her trim, green hedgerow,
Invade her garden, batter at her door?
Yet, even as she gazed, the militant meadow
Seemed to give forth a menacing deep roar . . .

Was it reality or fantasy? . . .
Felicity stood with slowly clearing vision,
Alive in tingling veins the prophecy
Of dream from which she was so newly risen.

"Sleep must be brief since worlds are dying fast,
New order rising through new deadly power."
With sinking heart she knew at poignant last,
Her cloistered beauty was but for an hour . . .

The trumpeting wind proclaimed a meadow lost,
Obliteration of things close and dear.
She bowed her head to certain holocaust,
Frail atom in a change too vast for fear.

ROSAMOND'S MAZE

(A legend)

"Rosamond the Fayre dyed at Woodstocke where King Henry had made for her a house of wonderful working, so that no man or woman might come to her but he that was instructed by the King. This house . . . was called Labyrinthus . . . wrought like unto a knot in a garden called a maze; but it was commonly said that lastly the queen came to her (Rosamond) by a clue of thridde or silk and so dealt with her that she lived not long: but when she was dead she was buried at Godstow in a house of nunnes." . . .

I. THE MAZE

It was wrought from living forest,
The marvelous maze,
Circling unknown turf
Where wild things graze;
Knotted from springing greenwood,
Fern, scented bush,
Elusive as the far notes
Of a flying thrush.

Winding in tunnels secret
Such as moles bore underground,
Or murmuring waters cover
With belovèd sound,
It led through broom and heather
Under a thorny hill,
Cunningly hid and guarded
As the whorl of a shell.

But in the glare of the day's heat
When nightingales ceased to exult,
And sun sucked at the flowers,
A king, sword bared to the hilt,
Yearning for his lost freedom
Strode there, drawn by a thread
Whose fragile silk found a bower
Soft as a fairy's bed.

With rose and musk it was sated,
Bee song wound thither at noon,
Where one sat within as fragrant
As herbs gathered under the moon.
Like a missal preciously handled
She drew him close to her,
(O hair, yellow as corn silk,
The winds lift and stir!)

(Gentle of touch, the hours
Passed by them side by side,
Ran smooth to heel as greyhounds
Where white hares hide.)

II. THE VISITOR

The king was gone with crafty speed—
His knight upon watch nodded, trembled,
Dreams were malefic, things dissembled.
Sinister a sign:
Thrice had a raven snatched at the strand
Of silken thread held fast in his hand,
Rosamond's clear eyeshine
Was dulled too as a pearl is dimmed
By salty sea water faintly rimmed.
"Listen," said the knight's ear, "take heed.
Why did a branch break in the wood
And the turtle dove cry so sore?
Never a living creature could
Find its way to this secret door.
Holy Virgin, evermore strike our enemies blind!
Someone comes indeed!
Robes rustle like northeast wind!"

The knight's eyeballs are streaked with red,
The lifeblood from his heart is drained,
He shudders, he stands like one enchained,
Overcome with withering dread,
As a muffled figure looms through the green,
Semblance of an angry queen.
(Here? Christ's mercy! here!
And life is very dear.)

"Yield up that ball of thread!"
Like pliant willow is he bent
And to her bidding he is lent,
As to the bower she strides straight
Consumed by a leaping flame of hate.
No questions asked
And her face is masked.
(Can Rosamond escape the snare?)
"Too late," sounds on the air,
"Too late!"

III. THE DRAUGHT

The sky is relentless as the cup,
The maple cup the sovereign holds.
And the draught within is green
As the marking of a snake,

Green as the slime of a water brake
When a desert traveler stoops low.
No purity of snow
Crusts the edges or cools the drink.
Watching bird turns head to blink
At the sweet world on the brink
Of desolate overthrow.
Then a cry lifts strong as that
Breaking from the newly born,
Entering on a life forlorn.
Hopeless as the horn
That spells a fortress taken,
A castle forsaken,
A love to mourn.
The empty cup is turnèd up. . . .

IV. THE TOMB

O then the bower whispered,
The sad leaves rustled;
When queen and knight were gone
The strong trees, one by one,
Bent and gazed upon the dead,
With love caressed her.

Birds of the forest dressed her
In new-grown buds and leaves,
From head to foot they tressed her,
Closing her eyes.
The trees regretful
Gathering here and there,
Wove a sweet-smelling bier of linden wood
Of beamy yellow for to rest her skull.
She lay in beauteous state
And fanciful,
Till lapped in lead
And borne away to Godstow nunnery.

The forest closed its eye.
Branches drew together
With gentle stir and quiver
As leaves after a sharp shower
Take counsel together.
From that day forth
No footfall printed the green ground.
East or west or north or south,
No traveler nor hound
In fair, foul weather,
By blowing scent of any flower,
Might spy out Rosamond's bower
Lost in the heather.

PLOD TORTOISE

Defeated man, when heart sinks low,
Lift it up, lean on your plough,
Observant of the season's ring;
Know by that oracle
The countless times delinquent Spring
That blooms for all her tarrying,
Nothing vigorous or full
Evolves at undue speed
Even at fiercest need.
Too early orchard smitten by the frost
Is proof. The blossom lost.
Perfection of a flower
Obtains through many a lull
Of many a waiting hour.
That tripping nymph, Expediency,
Is a poor handmaid for tortoise earth.
Before the birth
The darkling struggle of the child;
Before the warmth, the windswept wild
And hooded snow.
To grow, to grow,
Trickling sap mounts cautiously,
Bud scarce dares to wink an eye,
Life inches snailwise from curled leaf—
Then summer flashes, brilliant, brief.

There must be time, angelic time,
All of time is given you, man,
To mark with chalk the circle of your walk,
In your submission,
Spell the word fruition.

CPSIA information can be obtained at www.ICGtesting.com
Printed in the USA
LVOW12s2041151214

418944LV00001B/317/P

9 781417 992751